presented to

Mary

from

Melissa

on this date

Nov 15, 2005

Mother's Gifts to Me

DIANNA BOOHER

Published by J. Countryman, a division of Thomas Nelson, Inc.,
Nashville, Tennessee 37214. Published by J. Countryman.

Project Editor: Terri Gibbs

Illustrator: Gwendolyn Babbitt

Designed by Left Coast Design Inc. Portland, Oregon.

ISBN: 08499-5509-2

Published in consultation with the literary agency of

Alive Communications

1465 Kelly Johnson Blvd., Suite 320

Colorado Springs, CO

80920

Printed in the U.S.A.

www.jcountryman.com

To My Mother

Opal Schronk Daniels

and

- to all mothers who have loved their children
- to expectant mothers who want to grow children of character
- to stepmothers who have suddenly become one of the most important persons in a child's life

The God to whom little [girls] say
their prayers has a face very
much like their mother's.

SIR JAMES M. BARRIE

the power of forgiveness

I laid awake one very long night at the age of seven. As the school year wore on, my conscience grew heavier and heavier.

Every morning Mother would give me an extra nickel with my lunch money, telling me that I could spend the nickel for a Popsicle or ice cream only if I ate **all** my lunch first. I didn't eat all the lunch, but I typically spent my nickel. When I would come in from school, I always dreaded the days she remembered to ask pointedly, "Did you spend your nickel? Are you sure you ate a good lunch?" Sometimes I avoided the feeling of guilt when she phrased it that way, because even in my seven-year-old mind, I could rationalize that she had asked about eating "a **good** lunch," not "**all** my lunch." **Good** was relative; **all** was not.

But guilt got the better of me one particular evening. Mother kissed me, tucked me into bed, and left me in the darkness for my prayers. Head under the covers, I started to sniffle, then sob. When I finally called out for her, she came traipsing back into my room.

"I've got to tell you something," I said as I wiggled out from under the blanket.

She sat down beside me on the bed, eyes fixed on my face, concern in her expression.

I made my confession.

"I see," is all she said for a moment. Then, "Well, lying is wrong." I nodded agreement. "But I'm glad you told me. Have you asked God to forgive you?" I nodded again. "Good. Then He has . . . and, I forgive you, too." Instead of the anticipated spanking, she merely reached under the covers and pulled me up close for a hug.

Ten thousand pounds rolled off my tiny shoulders. Then I said to myself more than to her, "But I guess I still don't get any more nickels."

She swallowed a smile. "I think eating a **good** lunch rather than **all** your lunch will be good enough." With that, she hugged me again for good measure and left the room.

That was my first understanding of the power of forgiveness.

talking in the gaps

mother and I spent hours talking—without ever planning to. She was never one to come into my room, plop down on my bed, and say, "So tell me all about your day!" Instead, our habit was to do things together that provided gaps of time for us to share our thoughts with each other.

- When we cooked dinner together, she told me about how to test a cake for doneness.
- When we walked the cotton fields, hoe in hand hacking weeds, we discussed how best to divvy up my day's earnings to buy special treasures and realize college dreams.
- While we sloshed permanent solution on each other's hair and carefully rolled the strands, we talked about the difference between boy friends and boyfriends.
- As we folded clothes, we traded thoughts about how best to attack a demanding English assignment.
- When we walked the streets in search of size 5AA school shoes, we talked of husbandly attributes.

It was chatter with mother, scattered here and there in the gaps of life, that filled my life with great treasure.

memoraBLe conversations with moTHeR

R ecord here some of the lessons of life you learned from heart-to-heart talks with your mother—whether while piddling around or on purpose.

_____

_____

_____

_____

_____

_____

_____

_____

_____

_____

_____

_____

_____

Love-stamped

I am grateful to my mother for my own capacity to feel and receive love. With every word, touch, and action through all the routine chores of mothering, she set the pattern for unconditional love—concern, care, comfort and compassion.

> *Mother loved all mankind, but she did not know how to let her children love her.*
>
> ANNA ROOSEVELT

In turn, she knew how to accept love. It came to her in the form of bouquets of wild flowers, burned toast "just the way she liked it" on Mother's Day, cozy hugs when she had the flu, and cheap perfume from a teenager's earnings. As I look around my adult world, I see many men and women who have grown up without this emotional foundation and, therefore, have continuing difficulties with relationships of all kinds. The love my mother gave to me—and received so graciously from me—enables me in turn to love my family, friends, . . . and my world.

mothers have feelings

I never feel so ashamed and irritated with myself as when I say something insensitive that hurts my mother's feelings. The look of patience and humility on her face seeps from the deepest crevice in her heart. That expression of pain at once slices me with both regret and resolve to do better. Few offenses are more despicable than to wound a mother's heart.

taste-testing

By middle-age, most men and women remember their mothers as wonderful cooks. Truth of the matter, some mothers couldn't boil water. But mine—she was a tremendous cook. There were seldom hours in the day or money in the kitty for fancy gourmet meals, but she cooked the nutritious things we needed for a balanced diet, and she seasoned them with just the right knack. When I bounced into the house from play, school, or my part-time job, here are some of the things I looked forward to at dinner:

- Corn on the cob with lots of butter
- Steak grilled with barbecue sauce
- Chicken and dumplings
- Fried squash
- Crispy okra
- Chocolate pie
- Hot apple turnovers
- Banana pudding

If cleanliness is next to godliness, then cooking is surely next to motherliness.

C an you smell and taste it now—that favorite casserole
or those cookies your mother made so often? List the
favorite dishes that your mother prepared:

_____

_____

_____

_____

_____

_____

_____

_____

_____

_____

a s an author, I've read hundreds of books for pleasure and researched thousands of books for information. But my mother was the first book I read as a child, and I've checked her out of the library of my mind ever so many times during the intervening years of adulthood. She'll probably be the last book I read at my death.

The mother's heart is the child's schoolroom.

HENRY WARD
BEECHER

Clever men create
themselves, but clever women,
it seems to me, are created by their
mothers. Women can never quite escape
their mothers' cosmic pull, not their lip-
biting expectations or their faulty love. We
want to please our mothers, emulate them,
disgrace them, oblige them, outrage them,
and bury ourselves in the mysteries
and consolations of their presence.

CAROL SHIELDS

The Pledge of Allegiance states that we live under God's benevolence. Our country was founded on Christian principles, and uses the "In God We Trust" inscription on our coins to prove it. Congress prays to invoke God's wisdom for its day's work. My English teacher quoted Scripture along with Shakespeare in class discussions. Our community has a church on every corner.

In short, the concept of God somehow seeped into my consciousness along with the fact that water tasted good on a hot summer day and that the sun rose each morning. I don't remember when I did **not** know of God's existence.

But it was Mother who made God real and faith personal.

> *No man is poor who has had a godly mother.*
>
> ABRAHAM LINCOLN

- ⟲ At meals and during family devotions, she prayed for us individually as children, for her sick friends and for guidance about jobs and financial decisions.
- ⟲ She read her Bible every morning, day after day after day.
- ⟲ She hummed praise songs as she ironed.
- ⟲ She and Dad took us to church on Sundays, even when she wasn't feeling well or was tired.
- ⟲ She did the morally right thing in times of conflict.
- ⟲ She dealt with disappointment without despair.

Mother took God from a religious theory to a relationship right before my eyes.

my parents were in the balcony? At ten o'clock in the morning? On a Tuesday? During the work week? Then that was the best part of this National Honor Society thing. As a student transferring from a tiny B school to a 4-A district with 465 in our class, I was new to the whole concept. But I was delighted when the principal said into the microphone, "If you'll direct your attention to the balcony, you'll see that you were the last to know. We've contacted your parents and invited them to join us today in celebration of your achievements."

Who had instilled in us the importance of learning? Who had instilled the principle of always doing your best? Who had refused to let us go out to play until we finished our homework? Who had drilled us on the multiplication tables, the spelling words, and the state capitals?

It should have been no surprise—of course, Mom and Dad would be in the balcony!

No childhood achievement becomes complete without your mother looking on. No adult "news"—good or bad—becomes permanent until shared with your mother.

L ist some of the special times you were proud to have
your mother applauding your achievements:

_____

_____

_____

_____

_____

_____

_____

_____

_____

If you want your children to turn out well, spend twice as much time with them, and half as much money.

abigail
van buren

_____

_____

_____

_____

m other was both tolerant and inflexible.

- She was tolerant about how much dust I could leave on my bookshelves.
- She was inflexible about my learning to work.

- She was tolerant about what foods I ate at midnight on the school bus home from a basketball game.
- She was inflexible about cooking nutritious meals.

- She was tolerant about whom I chose as best friend of the week.
- She was inflexible about making me give Valentines to **everyone** in the class.

- She was tolerant about a low grade.
- She was inflexible about my doing homework and reviewing for a test.

- She was tolerant about which clothes I wore to school or a party.
- She was inflexible about modesty before any outfit came home from the store.
- She was tolerant about my dating—where I went and what time I came home.
- She was inflexible about knowing who I was with and what I was doing when I got there.

- She was tolerant about what I baked and how I baked it.
- She was inflexible about my learning skills that I'd need as a homemaker.

- She was tolerant about where I sat as a teenager in the church.
- She was inflexible about my being there.

- She was tolerant about where I got a part-time job for spending-money.
- She was inflexible about not having it interfere with school, church, or family activities.

- She was tolerant about how I spent my allowance.
- She was inflexible about tithing and saving.

- She was tolerant about my wild imagination and excited exaggerations over calamities.
- She was inflexible about my telling the truth.

- She was tolerant about my tales of woe about which mean kids and cruel teachers I did or didn't like.
- She was inflexible about my treating others with kindness and respect.

HOW to treat a man

mother demonstrated how to treat a husband to make him love and cherish her. She's been practicing with the same man for fifty-five years now.

On occasion, she coddles him—through colds and fever and with favorite casseroles. As if he were a king on his throne, she serves him bedtime snacks of popcorn and leftover pudding in front of the nightly news.

On occasion, she guides him like a child: She shops for his underwear, lays out ties to match his suits, and tells him when he needs a haircut. At other times, she does his bidding as if **he** were the parent, patiently running his errands to the dry-cleaners and the hardware store.

She isn't afraid to speak her mind to him about what investments will prove best for the long-haul—whether they should sell the rental property or if they should donate to the local fund-raiser. On the other hand, where his mistakes or shortcomings are concerned, she knows to hold her tongue in front of the kids and friends.

Mother has learned the fine art of negotiating. If they go to his favorite vacation spot this year, she gets to redecorate the kitchen next year.

She capably and charitably makes demands on his time. She knows when to obligate him to attend a child's piano recital, and when to let him roam free to hunt and fish with his buddies. She insists that he help with the housework and preparations for guests. She, in turns, helps clean the garage and wash the car.

She respects his judgment, praises him in front of family and friends, and follows his leadership in important family decisions.

In short, she accepts his authority without diminishing her own. The heart of her husband does safely dwell with her.

m y mother has been in perpetual motion
since she was wheeled out of the delivery
room. To attend four ballgames a
week, church services three
times a week, and at
least one community
function each week
took planning and
determination. My
earliest memories
include seeing my
mother hanging
clothes on the
clothesline at
dawn before she
left for work,
folding clothes
while she
cooked dinner, addressing

get-well cards at a ball game, canning beets while she drilled us on fractions, baking cookies for school while she prepared to teach her Sunday school class, and listening to the news while she mopped the floor. When others said they didn't have time to volunteer for this or that project, mother made time.

She modeled personal productivity that would make the experts pale. Can I do less?

By and large, mothers and housewives are the only workers who do not have regular time off. They are the great vacation-less class.

aNNe mORROW LINDBeRҪH

Cleaning your house while your kids are still growing is like shoveling the walk before it stops snowing.

pHYLLIs DILLeR

B efore my second child was born, the doctor sent me home to stay in bed for the final four months of the pregnancy. My instructions were for complete bed rest—not to sit up, not to stand. With a two-year-old already on the scene, our household had to make some necessary adjustments. My mother, with periodic relief from my mother-in-law, worked me and my family back into her daily routine. She cleaned the house, cooked our meals, washed our clothes, ran our errands, waited on me hand and foot, and chased her toddler grandson—all while keeping my dad and her own household running.

In short, she put her own life on hold for four months.

My most treasured memories of my mother are from such times of need. The time when I'd been jilted by a boyfriend. The time between anesthesia and surgery for a suspicious tumor. The time when I realized a broken marriage would not be repaired. The times when the weariness of unending travel and work overwhelms me.

Whether the need is physical or emotional, mothers are made for such times.

ist some situations, crises, or occasions when you've leaned heavily on your mother's emotional support or physical help and presence.

_____

_____

_____

_____

_____

_____

_____

_____

You never get over being a child, long as you have a mother to go to.

SARAH ORNE
JEWETT

_____

_____

_____

_____

_____

meddle moments

How very tempted our mothers must be—tempted to meddle in our marriages and in the way we raise our children and grandchildren. Tempted to tell us how to spend or not spend our money. Tempted to chastise us for not using our God-given talents and time wisely. Tempted to offer us advice when we did not ask for it.

Instead, they somehow manage to keep their mouths shut all through our adult years, and just be there for us, supporting us, giving guidance only when asked, and offering opinions only when solicited.

What courage our mothers have had simply to trust us to God's hands.

Father, may my children fulfill your plan and purpose for their lives. May the Spirit of the Lord be upon them—the Spirit of wisdom and understanding, the Spirit of counsel and of power, the Spirit of knowledge and of the fear of the Lord.

ISAIAH 11:2

Our children are not going
to be just our children they are
going to be other people's husbands
and wives and the parents
of our grandchildren.

DR. MARY CALDERONE

Nothing else will ever make you as
happy or as sad, as proud or
as tired, as motherhood.

ELIA PARSONS

strong and tender

my younger brother, Keith, had polio at
the age of two. He had just been
dismissed from Texas Scottish Rite Hospital for
Children in Dallas, and Mother and Dad had brought
him home to care for him, with instructions to give him
hot baths for his muscles.

Only moments after my mother dipped him into the hot
water for that first bath, his eyes closed and she could not rouse
him. She shook him and tugged at him, but he lay lifeless in the
tub. Grabbing him up in a blanket, she laid him in the backseat
of the car, and she and Dad sped off to the nearest doctor—
their family doctor who practiced in a rural community a half
hour away.

For the entire trip, mother sat stoically while Daddy kept his
eyes on the road and the speedometer over 100. They pulled
into the driveway of Dr. Girzzaffi's home, and Daddy jumped out
to summon his help. The doctor followed him back outside,
opened the car door, and pulled back the blanket. My brother
opened his eyes for the first time since he'd been slipped into the
bath water, and smiled.

Only after the doctor explained that the hot bath had simply put him into such deep relaxation that he'd gone to sleep, did my mother break into hysterical tears.

It was not the last time my mother displayed both strength and tenderness.

I've seen her cry when she overheard a street person asking for free food at a local restaurant and timidly tuck cash in his pocket. And I've seen her staunchly insist that a department store manager refund her money for a defective iron.

I've seen her wash and clothe an abused mother and small children. And I've seen her tell an itinerant troublemaker to get off our property.

In front of a PTA group, I've heard her speak her mind about an injustice and hold her tongue about an opinion.

The lessons weren't lost on me. Life is all about the right mixture of strength and tenderness of heart.

One mother achieves more
than a hundred teachers.

JEWISH PROVERB

O nce the "I Do's" were said, Mother demonstrated the same love and acceptance toward her sons-in-law and daughters-in-law that she showed to her own children. There are never unkind words to the child about the spouse. There are never exclusions when family secrets surface. There are never differences in the value of gifts given. There are never concerns expressed for one without the other. Should a stranger stumble into one of our family gatherings, he'd have a difficult time identifying the children from the children-in-law.

One of the greatest gifts mothers can give their children is warm acceptance and impartial love for their children's spouses.

Advice to mothers: Take off your earrings, your ring, your precious family heirloom, and give it to [your daughter-in-law] along with your love and trust. Trust and love are wonderful, but don't forget the earrings.

ESTEÉ LAUDER

taiLors aND tents

the customer glanced over my shoulder as she left my house, as if expecting to see a pup-tent model set up in my dining room. I was twenty-four years old at the time, with a toddler and a new baby. My husband and I had just moved to a new job in Boulder, Colorado, and it didn't take us long to realize that his salary wasn't going to cover the additional expense of a new baby. Having decided to stay home with my children during their early years, I'd set myself up in business as a custom tailor.

But sewing a tent—my mother had never prepared me for this.

At six o'clock the next morning, I stood hunched over the two pieces of plywood laid over two saw horses serving as my cutting table in the basement. A camping tent . . . where to start? As I pushed the scissors through the canvas, I hoped the tent would be easier than the ski parkas of the previous week.

My mind twitched between fear and gratitude. Fear that I couldn't do the job and gratitude that my mother's sewing lessons had given me the confidence to try. My mother had shown endless patience as she taught me to make my own clothes. Take out that tuck—the bodice is too tight. Rip out the sleeve—there's a pucker at the shoulder. Press open the seam, or the lining won't lie flat. Those tedious instructions had led to the current tent project.

That year's sewing income got us through a very tough spot. The pain and patience of do-overs aside, sewing has been a useful skill through the years.

My mother was right—there's value in any honest work and the willingness to do what you must to survive and make your way in the world.

H ow has your life been different because of some skill your mother taught you? What was that skill? Record how you felt learning that skill early in your life, as well as how you have profited since:

Whatever your hand finds to do, do it with all your might.

ecclesiastes 9:10

_____

_____

_____

_____

_____

_____

_____

_____

_____

_____

_____

_____

_____

S ome mothers never teach their daughters to sew or cook or decorate. But come to think of it, you can buy clothes, cookies, and decorator services. You can't buy love and values.

Record here some of the valuable things your mother gave you that you could never buy:

_____

_____

_____

_____

_____

_____

_____

_____

_____

Homes are built on the foundation of wisdom and understanding. Where there is knowledge, the rooms are furnished with valuable, learning things.

PROVERBS 24:3—4

Yelling at the top of our lungs, we hit the doorway after school every afternoon with, "Moooootheeeeer, I'm hooooommme." Sometimes just for the fun of it, Mother would tuck herself into a nook to hide. Then when we'd go lunging through the house looking for her and she'd step out and yell "boo."

I suspect she had enormous amounts of fun each day in the quiet before the storm.

Although we've long since dropped the "boo" part, I still stop by for a visit and find her enjoying the solitude. There's rarely any music playing in the background. The television is always off. She's not talking to friends on the phone. Instead, she's quietly working on one of her pet projects—flower arranging, painting ceramics, refinishing furniture, or learning to do spreadsheets on the computer.

Unlike those who seem uncomfort-

> *A baby enters your home and makes so much noise for twenty years you can hardly stand it—then departs, leaving the house so silent you think you'll go mad.*
>
> DR. J. a. HoLmes

able when they find themselves alone, she always discovers enjoyable ways to spend her time and use her mind. She taught me to be content with my own company.

Not to have to depend on others for peace of mind or food for thought grants great freedom.

CHOICES

m other created an environment where we as children and adults could grow unfettered by unreasoned guilt and unrealistic expectations. She allowed us to choose different jobs, addresses, and lifestyles than what she chose—without causing us to doubt our choices.

She respected our differences without seeing them as betrayals.

At every step the child should be allowed to meet the real experience of life; the thorns should never be plucked from his roses.

eLLen key

Children are likely to live up to what you believe of them.

LaDy bIRD JOHNSON

CHATTERING THE BATTER

I started playing girls' basketball on the school team in the fourth grade. Two nights a week during season . . . followed by volleyball . . . then cheerleading for football season. My brother played football in the fall, basketball in the winter, baseball and track in the spring. That meant that for most seasons Mother had a game commitment at least four nights a week, not to mention practice and tournaments.

Did she go grudgingly? Hardly. During football season, she yelled at the wide-receivers when they dropped the ball, applauded the defense when they forced a safety, and booed the refs for not calling clipping. During basketball season, she dreaded a tie-ball when my opponent was six feet tall, hoped for a one-and-one shot when I got fouled, and spotted a double-dribble a mile away.

> *It's good for a child to lose as well as win. They must learn in life they are going to be up today and maybe down tomorrow.*
>
> RUBY MIDDLETON FORSYTHE

During baseball season, she had her own opinions about when it was wise to bunt, yelled at the runner to tag up after a pop fly, and needled the batter on a three-and-two count.

In short, she spoke the language. She understood the importance of supporting our interests and joining in our activities wholeheartedly. When there was a rough spot in our relationship, she always knew how to reconnect the conversational crosswires with things that interested us.

Battleships and Barbies

a few years ago when my eighteen-year-old daughter came home from a weekend visit with my mother, I asked what they'd done.

"Tried on wedding dresses," she said as if that were the most common pastime for eighteen-year-olds and their grandmothers.

With a little probing, I discovered that her cousin Leanne had spent the weekend also, and they had talked their grandmother into driving them all around the Dallas-Fort Worth metroplex just to try on dresses and dream.

The older my mother gets, the more she plays. She plays Battleship with Courtney and I-Spy with Mason. Her eight-year-old and ten-year-old granddaughters are usually up for movies and pizza. She keeps a cache of dress-up clothes and old jewelry in the hall closet for drama demands. A few months back, she accompanied her twenty-year-old grandson to shop for a new computer.

Even as adults, few things gain higher priority than play with those you love. Play patches hearts together for eternity.

> *Don't let your children win every game they play. Show them how they can win.*
>
> ALBERTA ROBERTS

t he sounds of my childhood home communicated warmth and welcome: The old washing machine that thumped when my mom threw in the tennis shoes. The rumbling of the tractors in nearby fields that drifted in through the open windows. The thunder of mom's car as it bounced off potholes in the road on the way to school. The crunch of gravel as she pulled into the driveway. Hymns being hummed while she folded the clothes.

When her own parents and sisters phoned, the "not much" response to the "what're you doing?" greeting followed by her recitation of the day's activities and crises.

Lullabies. Quiet answers to my questions. Sound advice. Whether asking me to dust the furniture, telling me to add another spoonful of milk to the icing, or inquiring about my cough, mother's voice was and is security and sanity in a frantic world.

Mother's voice is calm and measured, not excitable. Even today when I answer my ringing phone, her voice deposits peace of mind into my emotional account.

W hat "sounds of mother" do you recall from childhood?

_____

_____

_____

_____

_____

_____

_____

_____

_____

_____

A mother's love is like an island. In life's ocean vast and wide, a peaceful, quiet shelter from the restless, rising tide.

HELEN STEINER RICE

mother was always the kind of person who made you do something until you were old enough to **want** to:

- She made us brush our teeth before bedtime, even if it was midnight and we were tired.

- She made us do our homework, even when it was too long and too hard.

- She made us write thank-you notes for all our birthday and Christmas gifts, even if the gift were inexpensive and something we didn't particularly like.

- She made us eat vegetables, even though we preferred pizza.

- She made us call home, even when "only babies" had to do that.

- She made us turn off the TV in the living room when someone came to visit.

- She made us apologize, even when it wasn't all our fault.

She made us get up and go to church, even when we'd had a late date the night before.

She made us visit older relatives, even when "there wasn't anything to do."

She made us save a portion of our allowance, even when "all the other kids" got to spend theirs.

She made us work, when "none of the other kids" had to.

We finally got to the age when we **wanted to.** Funny how that happens. Self-discipline is often mother-discipline first.

caught between worry and anger

atching your mother in midair between worry and anger can be most reassuring. Do you recall those times when you did something foolish like fall off a motorcycle? Your mother worried to death that you'd hurt yourself badly—then after discovering the injury was minor, she scolded you for disobedience?

One night I told my mother I'd be home at eleven after a church youth meeting. When the meeting unexpectedly finished at nine, I decided to make up the difference by accepting an invitation to go out with an old boyfriend for hamburgers. When a friend's mother called mine and happened to mention that the meeting had ended at nine, my mother was sure I'd been left for dead along some deserted stretch of highway. When I pulled into our driveway at eleven, she burst out the backdoor toward me with eyes wild, "What's wrong? What happened?"

"Nothing. I went out for a hamburger with Don."

The fright drained from her eyes and fury took its place.

"You didn't call.
Your dad's been out
looking for you for two
hours!"

"Why? I told you I'd be home by
eleven. It's just now eleven.
How was I going to know
you'd worry?"

She wasn't to be swayed
by the logic of a teenager.

She'd insisted that my dad drive
every conceivable route between the
church and our house.

"Just wait till your dad gets back.
You're in big trouble!"

I went to bed that night, like my mother, caught
between two emotions: anger at the "unfair" punishment
and relief over my parents' love and protection.

> *To describe my
> mother would be
> to write about a
> hurricane in its
> perfect power.*
>
> maya angelou

tHe "JUDY" PROBLeMS IN MY WORLD

How to respond to Judy? The young friend of mine was always jealous because school work seemed to come easier for me than for her. To try to even the score, she teased and taunted me on the playground. When I came home in tears about the "Judy problem", Mother always listened and offered suggestions and comforting comments to lessen the hurt.

She never minimized the situation. She never demanded that I see the world from her point of view. Instead, she always tried to see the world from mine.

> *Don't let these parenting years get away from you. Your contributions to your children and grandchildren could rank as your greatest accomplishments in life.*
>
> DR. JAMES DOBSON

depending on mother

as a **child**, I depended on Mother for the physical things: food, clean clothes, a warm bed, an aspirin when I had a fever.

As an **adolescent,** I depended on her for instruction and boundaries: issues of etiquette, guidance about grades and graduation, encouragement for dealing with pimples and proms, discipline and corrections on wrong attitudes and dangerous habits, models for friendship and dating.

As an **adult,** I depend on her for courage, calm, comfort:

- the courage to stay on this emotional roller coaster called life.
- the calmness that comes from knowing that if she has handled whatever crisis and has lived to laugh about it, I can too.
- the comfort that she's praying for me in every decision and situation.

Every mother
is like Moses.
She does not enter
the promised land.
She prepares a world
she will not see.

POPE PAUL VI

W hen the store clerk gave us too much change, Mother made us give it back.

When other teens sneaked into the movies or the amusement park on a child's pass, Mother made us tell our true age.

When somebody lost something and I found it, my mother made me try to find the owner or turn it into the Lost and Found.

When I flunked a pop-quiz because I refused to cheat while friends did and got an "A," Mother complimented me on my decision.

When I helped someone else cheat because it was easier than being teased for being selfish with the answers, Mother punished me just as if the fault lay totally with me.

When I didn't know what to say in a babysitting situation about a child's behavior, my mother suggested the truth with tact.

The roots of honesty grow deep and early. They aren't easily pulled up in the winds of corporate bribes, political positioning, or customer finagling.

The
noblest calling in the
world is that of mother. True
motherhood is the most beautiful of
all arts, the greatest of all professions. She
who can paint a masterpiece or who can write
a book that will influence millions deserves the
plaudits and admiration of mankind; but she
who rears successfully a family of healthy, beautiful
sons and daughters whose immortal souls will be
exerting an influence throughout the ages long
after paintings shall have faded, and books
and statues shall have been destroyed,
deserves the highest honor
that man can give.

DAVID O. MCKAY

mother treats family like company

mother goes all out for kids and grandkids. During each holiday season (July 4th and Valentine's Day included), she hauls out the appropriate decorations and recipes and prepares as if the Pope were coming to visit. Never mind that no one but the family will see it all. Every time we sit down to her dining table as a family with whatever placemats, napkins, and dishes she has chosen for the occasion, we feel special. We count.

On the other hand, I've walked into the kitchen to find company sitting at a table of dirty dishes. A friend had called to say she was running late leaving work and needed to be at the school by 6:30 for a parent-teacher conference. Because we lived a couple of blocks from the school, mother invited her to drop by for a drive-off bologna sandwich and a paper towel full of chips on the way.

And many times a pastor of ours, single at the time, made it a point to drop by our house unexpectedly at dinner time. If we were eating leftovers, he forked into his share just like the rest of us.

In short, Mother treats her family like company and her company like family.

experts tell us we have more than 177 messages coming to us each day by phone, e-mail, paper, or media ads. Obviously, repetition is what counts—in selling, supervising, or sharing your life with kids.

Truisms from the mouths of mothers have shaped the lives of children from generation to generation. Here are some of my mother's favorites:

- Mothers have eyes in the back of their head.
- A little bird told me.
- Pretty is as pretty does.
- If you don't have time to do it right the first time, how will you ever have time to do it over?
- If anything's worth doing, it's worth doing well.
- Just do your best—that's all anybody can expect of you.
- The early bird gets the worm.
- Elbow grease works well.
- Early to bed, early to rise, makes a person healthy, wealthy, and wise.
- Honesty is the best policy.
- What no one else sees, God always does.

C an you hear your mother now? List here some of the
sayings she repeated to you during your growing-up years.

_____

_____

_____

_____

_____

_____

_____

_____

_____

*Some are kissing mothers and some are
scolding mothers, but it is love just the same,
and most mothers kiss and scold together.*

PEARL S. BUCK

frugal fun

W aste has never been in Mother's vocabulary.
I have probably forgotten all the times she pulled
items out of her bag of tricks to teach us how to live royally
yet within our means. There was the recycled sofa loaned to
us for our first home . . . the microwave that went to her
grandson's dorm room . . . the silk flowers revived from an
old wall wreath and rearranged for the dining table of her
granddaughter's new apartment . . . the dollar-off amusement
park tickets collected for her grandchildren's weekend enter-
tainment . . . the new bed sheet sewn into an elegant dust
ruffle for her daughter-in-law's guest bed. There were multiple
stops for groceries, because milk and bread were cheaper at
Kroger's while cheese and cereal were cheaper at Winn-Dixie.

In a world that encourages debt, she taught us money
management principles that gave us financial freedom for life.

*Ask your child what he wants for
dinner only if he is buying.*

FRAN LEBOWITZ

I t wasn't exactly a rare day when Mother came home from work and refereed a heated discussion between my brother and me. She usually began the refereeing with something like, "All right, one at a time. Who did what?"

> Children require guidance and sympathy far more than instruction.
>
> ANONYMOUS

"He hit me."

"I hit her because she called me a name."

"I called him a name because he wouldn't stop . . ."

And the explanation went on. And on. And on. Mother took the time to listen and establish the pattern of unraveling a tangled situation. She heard both of us out. She prevented the loudest mouth or the saddest story from always winning. She sorted fact from opinion and intention. She helped us develop options.

And the most dreaded part: "Now, you and your brother hug each other and say you're sorry. You're going to need each other someday."

It all came true. And we learned a lot about listening, anger, conflict resolution, apologizing, and forgiving— all skills and attitudes that have come in handy almost every day of our lives.

H ard work is, well, hard work. Mother often worked the cotton fields alongside Dad while we played in the dirt on the end rows. But because she was mother, she got to leave the field a half hour earlier than anybody else—to prepare lunch or dinner for the rest of us.

After we moved off the farm, she took an "easier" office job that kept her busy only eight to five. The rest of her hours were "free" to sponsor school events, watch ball-games, and wash dishes for our family of five. For a "hobby," she often sewed until midnight to make our clothes or create Christmas gifts.

> *The phrase "working mother" is redundant.*
>
> JANE SELLMAN

Watching Mother at work taught me the pleasure of creativity, the energy from staying in good physical condition, the satisfaction of doing something well, and the appreciation of those who benefit from the effort.

I called Mother one morning to say hello before I went to work. She had just returned from the grocery store with eight heads of lettuce, six pounds of carrots, ten bunches of scallions, and radishes galore. Why? She planned to make salad all day—it was her turn to help cook and serve at the homeless shelter that evening.

According to my mother's model, service to God and fellow human beings is not over when one retires. There's no such thing as growing too old to serve—whether it be by praying for those around you or ladling their gravy.

> *Giving kids clothes and food is one thing but it's much more important to teach them that other people besides themselves are important, and that the best thing they can do with their lives is to use them in the service of other people.*
>
> DOLORES HUERTA

All children love their mothers and see them larger than life. But it's through the eyes of an adult that we examine our own upbringing and begin to get a more balanced view. Happily, in my case, that childlike assessment of my mother hasn't changed through the years. As she approaches her sunset years and I follow her through the cycle of mothering and grandmothering, my appreciation of her work and wisdom grows. Even through the filter of adulthood, she still looms larger than life.

Only if my own children still give their upbringing high marks when they arrive at middle-age will I have a true measure of my contributions to their life. Mothering stripped of its sentiment matters most.

> When I stopped seeing my mother with the eyes of a child, I saw the woman who helped me give birth to myself.
>
> NANCY FRIDAY

m other spoke loudest when she was silent. When I made a catty remark about someone, Mother just looked at me.

When I told her about my weekend with a girlfriend and left out an incriminating incident—she just looked at me.

When I promised that I would finish the chores if I could just "wait a little while longer,"—she just looked at me.

When I announced my plans to spend lavishly on a fad—she just looked at me.

When I complained that I couldn't learn something or ever do it right—she just looked at me.

Somehow, I always "heard" her loud and clear.

CONSISTENCY COUNTS

S ome people measure their mother's love and devotion by her passion, often passion focused on one purpose. A mother may have a passion for ensuring that her son learn to play the piano. A mother may have a passion that her daughter study hard enough to graduate first in her class from Harvard. A mother may have a passion that her twins become the best of friends rather than just siblings. A mother may have a passion about fashion, safe schools, educational TV, public policy, or any number of good things.

But passion is not enough to raise kids today, because when the passion wanes, their attention dissolves. The

If you want your child to accept your values when he reaches his teen years, then you must be worthy of his respect during his younger days.

DR. JAMES
DOBSON

fact is, passion pales when compared to continuing, all-encompassing, sacrificial love. Love demonstrated despite feelings of the moment. Sure, there are times when I feel tired, lonely, and unappreciated. Sure, there are times when my own children hurt my feelings by things they say or do—or don't say or don't do. But Mother's love through the years remains my criteria for judging my own love's strength and consistency.

One of the most important things Mother taught me was how to get along without her.

She taught me to meet my physical needs: I could cook for myself and the family by the fourth grade.

She taught me to be resourceful by finding what I needed to meet a demanding teacher's assignments.

She taught me to save my money by giving me the freedom to spend it—on something I didn't really want and would regret within hours.

She taught me to stand up for myself with the bullies on the playground.

She taught me to make my own decisions by supplying the guidelines and giving me latitude within those boundaries of rules and reason.

She taught me the value of friendships, especially in moments of crisis.

Although I'm grateful God has granted my mother long life, her greatest gift to me was preparation early in life to live without her.

favorite family stories

L ike flour, sugar, and salt, family jokes and stories are staples around our house.

Mother likes to tell about her target practice. One evening when we were away from home, a drunk broke into our house and made himself at home. So the next day, Dad bought Mother a pistol to keep for protection. Problem was, Mother had never shot a gun before. The following day a car full of yelling migrant workers came speeding up the gravel road leading to our farmhouse. Frightened from the recent break-in, she grabbed us kids into the bedroom with her, pulled out the pistol, and started shooting through the roof to scare them away. They kept driving . . . and Dad sold the gun the next day.

Mothers keep such stories alive for families. They build history, memories, and bonds.

W hat story do you remember hearing over and over in your family?

_____

_____

_____

_____

_____

_____

_____

_____

_____

_____

_____

_____

_____

mothers are not friends

I'm so glad Mother was my mother and not my friend . . .

Friends encourage you in what you plan to do.
Mothers question you about what you plan to do.

Friends come over when there's fun; they go
   home when there's work.
Mothers pay for the fun and stay for the work.

Friends love you for the good times.
Mothers love you during the bad times.

Friends help you break the rules to free you.
Mothers make the rules to shape you.

Friends talk to you about their problems.
Mothers listen to you talk about your problems.

Friends join you in your search for answers.
Mothers model the answers to your search.

needs and wants

mother taught me to separate wants from needs. The TV bombards us with a case for a new car. The women's magazines tease us with the season's new styles. The Classified Ads tempt us with a change in salary. A friend's new house makes our own look dowdy.

As a young adult away from home for the first time and existing on my own paycheck, I recall often commenting to my mother that I **needed** this or that thing. She'd always flash an amused smile and reflect my choice of words back to me, **"Need?"** It was a reminder that "wants" often cloud our perspective about true needs.

Had it not been for that habit of hers, I'm sure I would have been in debt up to my elbows by the time I was twenty-five.

Mommy
herself has told us
that she looked upon us
more as her friends than her
daughters. Now that is all very
fine, but still, a friend can't take a
mother's place. I need my mother
as an example which I can follow.
I want to be able to respect her.

anne frank

A torn jacket is
soon mended, but hard
words bruise the heart of a child.

HENRY WADSWORTH LONGFELLOW

A mother is not a person
to lean on but a person to
make leaning unnecessary.

DOROTHY CANFIELD FISHER

Sometimes the poorest woman
leaves her children the
richest inheritance.

RUTH E. RENKEL

mother laid the groundwork for a close-knit family. And close has little to do with distance. Our family now lives close enough to allow all eighteen of us to routinely gather together as one big family in times of need or celebration. But that's not always been the case. The intimacy has more to do with the head than the highway.

> *What would I want on my gravestone for posterity? "Mother."*
>
> JeSSICa LaNGe

Mother loves us all individually, but treats us all equally.

She never repeats one child's secrets, business, or dreams to another without their permission.

She never "wonders" aloud why a certain family member acts, or says, or does a peculiar thing.

She has no favorites, yet she makes each one of our clan feel individually special by cooking their favorite food on a holiday or remembering to ask about their difficult project on hold.

Close-knit families serve
to insulate members from
the chill of isolation in a
technologically-wired world.
Nearness and distance are
conditions of the heart.

*If you
bungle raising
your children, I don't
think whatever else you
do well matters very much.*

JACQUELINE
KENNEDY ONASSIS

Raising the Bar

O ne Saturday morning I finished my chores in record time so I could go out with my friends. When mother noticed I was getting ready to leave, she questioned me, "Did you finish dusting already? In ten minutes?"

"I did."

"Everywhere? Did you do it well?

"I did."

She made a quick inspection; the dusting work didn't pass. Neither did the ironing. "These shirts aren't ironed well either. Look at those wrinkles. You have to give the steam enough time to penetrate. You don't just swipe the iron over them and run." She said it as if I should know—after all, it wasn't the first time I'd heard it.

High standards surface two feelings: a feeling of not being able to measure up and a sense of great accomplishment when you do. Focusing on the latter builds self-confidence and makes future bosses proud.

a jump on the competition

mother followed me all the way to the door the evening I left on Daddy's arm to attend the FFA banquet at the school. She tagged along, not to say goodbye—but to finish the hem in my dress. Only four days before the event, the sponsor caught me in the hallway to say, "I don't think I mentioned it yet, but as the chapter sweetheart you're invited to the banquet on Friday night."

The news delighted me; it meant I would be the only girl in a roomful of teenage boys. But my mother panicked. "What'll you wear? We'll have to find something quick." She was working outside our home at the time, so she picked me up from school the next evening to shop for fabric and then sewed late into the night for two evenings to finish the dress.

Daddy beamed with pride to be my invited escort for the evening. Mother wished us fun on the way out the door.

Although my mother has always been beautiful and vivacious, she never tried to compete with me. If the

family could afford only one new dress for the season, I got it. If the budget would allow limited spending-money for an outing, I had the opportunity to go, do, and see. If someone offered a learning opportunity during the summer break, I became the student.

It was as if she understood that the future would hold competition enough in every other arena of life—for the best grades, for the best universities, for the best job. She intended to give me a head start with no one else on the starting line.

BONDS AND BAND-AIDS

mother took the time to build traditions for our family—bonds that build intimacy and Band-Aids that ease the pain. At Christmas, one of our traditions is for the entire clan to gather and watch while each child takes part in "putting on a program" before we unwrap gifts—either quoting Scripture, singing a song, performing a play, or reciting a poem.

Another tradition is playing table games at family get-togethers—from Forty-Two to Yahtze to Trivial Pursuit, both young and old pit their luck and wits around the dining table.

We show up for each other's celebrations—birthdays, graduations, baptisms, weddings.

Another funny tradition is circulating old, serviceable furniture and equipment. Whoever's child is staking out a college dorm or renting a first apartment makes the rounds to collect cast-aways from the various households—a lamp here, a can opener there.

Mothers create traditions that hold families together through the tough spots.

your family traditions and rituals

L ist the traditions and rituals you enjoy in your family
and what part your mother played in establishing or
encouraging those. Consider why each has been important
in the life of your family:

_____

_____

_____

_____

_____

_____

_____

_____

_____

_____

_____

_____

GIVING AS GOOD

mother is a giver rather than a taker. She
models the joy of giving time,

tithe,

treasured possessions,

thanks,

attention,

patience,

praise,

prayer,

loyalty,

laughter,

and love.

When I give, I feel most like her.

A beautiful woman
appeals to the eye;
a good woman
appeals to the
heart. One is
a jewel, the
other a
treasure.

NAPOLEON
BONAPARTE

I really
learned
it all from
mothers.

BENJAMIN
SPOCK

UNPOPULAR OPINIONS

mother was master of the unpopular opinion.

- She understood that the world was filled with physical dangers and moral pitfalls.
- She refused to believe it was "perfectly safe" for me to walk or drive the streets alone at midnight.
- She disapproved of sex before marriage.
- She saw no good to come of drinking alcohol.
- She feared mind-altering drugs.
- She doubted I had a strong need to attend unchaperoned parties.
- She insisted I had no one to blame for my failures but my lack of goals or discipline.

For all these strong opinions, she had the patience to listen to me argue the point. She had the strength of character to practice what she preached. She took the time to enforce the boundaries.

And most important, she had the courage to persist in these unpopular opinions until I came to them myself.

mothers aren't perfect. Mine wasn't. Sometimes she failed to say "I believe in you" when I wanted to hear it. Sometimes she was too distracted with her own worries or problems to ask me about my day or activities. Sometimes she was too tired to play or talk to me about boyfriend problems. Sometimes she scolded me for accidents that I didn't mean to cause.

> *The ideal mother, like the ideal marriage, is a fiction.*
>
> MILTON R. SAPIRSTEIN

But that doesn't lessen my love for her or her love for me. It makes her a human being who can identify with my own past and future shortcomings.

Life is about filtering out the negatives and focusing on the positives —the best formula yet devised for finding true contentment as an adult.

There was never
a great man who had
not a great mother.

OLIVE SCHREINER

I think togetherness is a very
important ingredient to family life.

BARBARA BUSH

No matter how old a mother is
she watches her middle-aged children
for signs of improvement.

FLORIDA SCOTT-MAXWELL

Acknowledgments for Quotations

Booher, Dianna. **8005 Quotes, Speeches, & Toasts.** Software based on the works of Dianna Booher and others. Austin, Texas: ModelOffice, Inc., 1996.

Cory, Lloyd. **Quotable Quotations**. Wheaton, Illinois: Victor Books, 1980.

Eisen, Armand. **For a New Mother.** Kansas City, Kansas: Andrews and McMeel, 1995.

Habel, Jennifer. **For Mom**. White Plains, New York: Peter Pauper Press, 1992.

Hansen, Debbie. **For Mother: A Bouquet of Sentiments**. Glendale Heights, Illinois: Great Quotations Publishing Company, 1993.

Honneger, Roy. **Mother, I Love You**. Glendale Heights, Illinois: Great Quotations Publishing Company, 1997.

_____. **My Daughter, My Special Friend.** Glendale Heights, Illinois: Great Quotations Publishing Company, 1997.

McKenzie, E. C. **14,000 Quips and Quotes for Writers & Speakers**. New York: Greenwich House, 1980.

Rando, Caterina. **Words of Women: Quotations for Success**. Software. San Francisco, California: Power Dynamics Publishing, Inc., 1995.

Safire, William and **Leonard Safire**. **Good Advice: More Than 2,000 Quotations to Help You Live Your Life**. New York: Wing Books, 1982.

_____. **With Love to A Special Mother**. Grand Rapids, Michigan: Fleming H. Revell, 1995.